12/15

D0934603

25

SPOTLIGHT ON NATIVE AMERICANS

MUSCOGEE (CREEK)

Ralph Waterby

PowerKiDS
press™

New York

Published in 2016 by The Rosen Publishing Group, Inc.
29 East 21st Street, New York, NY 10010

First Edition

Editor: Karolena Bielecki
Book Design: Kris Everson
Reviewed by: Robert J. Conley, Former Sequoyah Distinguished Professor at Western Carolina University and Director of Native American Studies at Morningside College and Montana State University
Supplemental material reviewed by: Donald A. Grinde, Jr., Professor of Transnational/American Studies at the State University of New York at Buffalo.

Photo Credits: Cover © Journal-Courier/Steve Warmowski/The Image Works; pp. 4–5 sebatl/E+/Getty Images; pp. 6, 9, 13 (right), 14, 19, 21, 23, 25 (right), 29 Native Stock; p. 7 MPI/Archvie Photos/Getty Images; pp. 10–11 Hulton Archive/Archive Photos/Getty Images; p. 13 (left) Peter Newark's American Pictures; pp. 16–17 © iStockphoto.com/MilosJokic; p. 25 (left) Corbis; p. 27 © iStockphoto.com/tacojim.

Library of Congress Cataloging-in-Publication Data

Waterby, Ralph.
Muscogee (Creek) / Ralph Waterby.
    pages cm. — (Spotlight on Native Americans)
 Includes bibliographical references and index.
 ISBN 978-1-4994-1650-3 (pbk.)
 ISBN 978-1-4994-1651-0 (6 pack)
 ISBN 978-1-4994-1653-4 (library binding)
 1. Creek Indians. 2. Creek Indians—History—Juvenile literature. 3. Creek Indians—Social life and customs—Juvenile literature. I. Title.
 E99.C9W375 2015
 975.004'97385—dc23
                                        2015007812

Manufactured in the United States of America

CPSIA Compliance Information: Batch #WS15PK: For Further Information contact Rosen Publishing, New York, New York at 1-800-237-9932

CONTENTS

ORIGINS OF THE MUSCOGEE

CHAPTER 1

About fifty-five thousand people are members of the Muscogee (Creek) **Nation**, the fourth-largest Native American nation in the United States. *Creek* is the name Europeans gave the Native Americans they found living along the waters of the Southeast in the late 1600s. Today, however, these Native Americans prefer the term their ancestors used—*Muscogee*.

Many Muscogee reside within the nation's eleven counties in east-central Oklahoma. Others live across the United States.

Early ancestors of the Muscogee were part of the vast Mississippian **culture**, which arose about A.D. 800 and extended over much of the Southeast and middle

of the continent. At its height, the Mississippian culture may have included 6.7 million people. The Muscogee first lived along the Ocmulgee River in present-day central Georgia and later spread to western Georgia and east-central Alabama.

The Muscogee origin story says they descended from the Cussitaw people. The Cussitaws climbed out of Earth's mouth and settled nearby. The Earth shook, roared, and ate some Cussitaw children, so the Cussitaws moved away, some east toward the rising sun. They followed a red river and found a mountain with a great fire on top. The Cussitaws helped themselves to this fire. The Muscogee have kept it burning ever since.

From the late 1500s through the early 1800s, many Muscogee people lived along the beautiful Chattahoochee River that runs through present-day Atlanta, Georgia. Men and boys arose at dawn to catch some of the river's many fish.

THE MUSCOGEE UNION
CHAPTER 2

To the uneducated eyes of the Europeans who had come to North America in the late 1500s and 1600s, the Muscogee appeared to be a single people. Instead they were a union of tribes that included the Muscogee, Alabama, Coasati, Hitchiti, Mikasuki, Apalachee, Natchez, Yuchi, and Shawnee peoples. The Muscogee made up the most numerous and powerful tribe in the union.

Early ancestors of the Muscogee built large ceremonial mounds. This one, near Okmulgee, Georgia, reminds visitors that a thriving culture existed in North America long before Europeans arrived.

Apalachee snake design circa 1500

Union member tribes were called tribal towns. Each town had its own chief and council. Its members spoke a version, or dialect, of the Muscogee language. Although the dialects differed somewhat from one town or tribe to the next, members could understand one another.

As towns grew and the land could no longer support the population, some of the people left and formed new settlements. Over time, as settlements increased, and the larger Muscogee towns took over smaller, non-Muscogee tribal towns, the union grew into what became known as the Creek **Confederacy**.

EUROPEAN CONTACT AND TRADING

CHAPTER 3

By the 1700s, traders, explorers, and settlers from Great Britain, France, and Spain were in North America. Almost all the Europeans treated the Native Americans poorly if not brutally. Soldiers and settlers commonly burned Muscogee towns to create room for new settlements. The warriors of the Creek Confederacy, however, were often able to defend their towns.

Britain, France, and Spain each wanted the Muscogee's goods for themselves. The leaders of the Upper and Lower Creeks feared that trading with only one country would lead to the other countries waging war against them. To decide what to do, the leaders formed a National Council, which agreed that trading with all three countries would offer the Muscogee the most protection against war.

Trading with all three countries, however, did not stop land loss. As more Europeans began settling in North America, they continued attempts to seize

The Europeans mainly wanted deerskins, for which they would pay a high price, from the Muscogee. In exchange, the Europeans gave the Muscogee beads, guns, metal tools, European clothes, and copper and tin pots.

Muscogee land. The 1773 Treaty of August gave up, or ceded, a large portion of Muscogee land in present-day Georgia to Great Britain. These lands became the first British colony in Georgia. What little land the Muscogee kept fell within the boundaries of the new United States at the end of the American Revolution in 1783.

THE CREEK CIVIL WAR
CHAPTER 4

In the early 1800s, the Shawnee Indian prophet Tecumseh urged Native Americans to rise up against white people. Whites would seize all Native American land and destroy Native American culture, he argued. The Upper Creeks agreed with Tecumseh. The Lower Creeks, however, believed that adopting white ways would lessen whites' hostility to natives and would ensure the Native Americans' survival.

More differences between the Upper and Lower Creeks surfaced. In the War of 1812 between Great

Britain and the United States, the Upper Creeks sided with Great Britain, while the Lower Creeks sided with the United States. These differences led to the Creek **Civil War** in 1813. Under their chief, William McIntosh, the Lower Creeks defeated the Upper Creeks in the Battle of Horseshoe Bend, along the Tallapoosa River. By the time the Lower Creeks had won the war in 1814, between two thousand and three thousand Muscogee, most of them from the Upper region, had died. The power of the Creek Confederacy had been broken.

In its war against Great Britain in 1812, the United States had help from Lower Creek warriors. Here, Tecumseh fights for Great Britain. This divide contributed to the Creek Civil War a year later.

LOSS OF LAND AND INDIAN REMOVAL

CHAPTER 5

In 1824, the United States offered to buy all of the Muscogee's land in Georgia and two-thirds of their land in Alabama. Acting on their own, rather than on behalf of the National Council, Lower Creek leader William McIntosh and several tribal chiefs accepted the offer and signed the Treaty of Indian Springs. Signing a treaty without council approval broke Muscogee law, and the National Council persuaded the United States to cancel the treaty.

The council suspected, however, that the United States would eventually force all Native Americans off the land. With council permission, Upper Creek leader Opothle Yahola signed the Treaty of Washington in 1826. Those who wanted to could stay in Alabama, but most Muscogee, including McIntosh's followers, moved west to Indian Territory in what is now Oklahoma.

The Indian Removal Act of 1832 called for Native Americans from the five largest tribes in the Southeast—

(Left) Lower Creek leader William McIntosh broke tribal law by signing a treaty without council permission. He was put to death for his crime. *(Right)* The Muscogee walked the 800-mile (1,300-km) trip to Indian Territory in today's Oklahoma. Nearly thirty-five hundred people died along the way.

the Muscogee, Choctaws, Cherokees, Chickasaws, and Seminoles—to voluntarily move to Indian Territory. Those who did not go voluntarily were forced to go. Under orders from President Andrew Jackson, the U.S. Army marched nearly twenty thousand Muscogee to Indian Territory during the harshest part of the winter of 1836 to 1837.

THE AMERICAN CIVIL WAR
CHAPTER 6

During the 1860s, the Civil War between the northern Union states and the southern Confederate states nearly destroyed the Muscogee's new unity.

Highly respected Upper Creek Chief Opothle Yahola served the Muscogee well before and after the forced removal of Native Americans from the Southeast to Indian Territory. He encouraged the Muscogee to honor and maintain their traditional ways.

In 1861, Daniel McIntosh, son of William McIntosh, supported the Confederate states. He formed a **regiment** to battle the Upper Creek Muscogee who had remained loyal to the Union. To avoid conflict, the aging Opothle Yahola tried to lead nearly three thousand Muscogee, Seminole, and Shawnee people out of Indian Territory into Kansas. Three battles with McIntosh and his Confederate troops, as well as a terrible blizzard, killed almost all of the Upper Creeks, including Yahola. Because of these attacks, many of the Upper Creeks joined the Union forces.

Even though the Upper Creeks had fought on the Union side, after the Civil War, the United States government forced the Creek Nation as well as the Choctaws, Cherokees, Chickasaws, and Seminoles to give up all their lands in the western part of Indian Territory.

After the Civil War, rivalries among the Muscogee died down. In 1867, the Muscogee passed a new **constitution** that created a two-house legislature, a court system, and a principal chief. The tribal town of Okmulgee was chosen as the capital.

AN ABUNDANT LIFE

CHAPTER 7

Before the Muscogees' first contact with Europeans in the mid-1500s and for two centuries more, **abundance** marked their lives. Muscogee lived near rivers and streams on fertile, easily farmed land that produced corn, beans, rice, sweet potatoes, and squash. By hunting deer, bear, turkey, wild birds, and rabbits, men provided ample food for their tribe. Women and children rounded out the Muscogee diet by gathering wild plants, nuts, berries, and roots. Button snakeroot, ginseng, and red cedar plants were used for medicines.

It may have been this abundance that shaped the Muscogee's thinking about ownership. Every tribal member enjoyed equal rights to the soil and what it produced, to the hunt and what it yielded, and even to household items. If one tribal member were to visit another member's house and say, "I need that knife," it would be freely given. All Indians were considered part of one family, and all men were called brother.

Creek women grew corn, along with squash and beans, in the Muscogees' communal gardens, which provided food for the entire village.

POLITICS AND SOCIETY
CHAPTER 8

Each town had its own chief who commanded respect and power. His council included a war chief, warriors, and hunters. The chief held a daily council meeting. Councils decided where to house the food supply, when to hold ceremonies, and when to wage war. Every meeting started with drinking a ceremonial tea. While the Europeans described it as "the black drink" because of its color, the Muscogee called it "the white drink" because of its purpose—to make the mind and spirit pure, or white.

Religious ceremonies also took place in the town square as did stickball, a game much like modern-day lacrosse. Called "the little brother of war," stickball offered exercise and friendly competition. It was also used to settle land disputes between tribes and clans.

Family compounds surrounded the square and spread out for several miles along rivers and streams. Compounds included a house for storing food, as well

When geese flew south, traditional Muscogee men knew winter would soon arrive. To protect against harsh weather, they built homes out of tree limbs, bark, and plant fibers.

as rectangular summer and winter homes. House frames consisted of poles made from wood or woven plant fibers. The walls were made of mud and straw and the roofs built of tree bark. Animal hides **insulated** the winter houses.

THE THREE WORLDS
CHAPTER 9

Traditional Muscogee believed that the universe was made up of three worlds—"This World," "The Upper World," and "The Under World." Humans, plants, and animals lived in This World.

The Upper World housed the Moon and Sun, as well as beings that looked like humans but could change shapes. Just beneath This World lay the Under World, home of ghosts and monsters.

The Muscogee tried to maintain a balance between the Upper and Under Worlds by keeping elements of the Upper and Under Worlds apart. Fire came from the Sun in the Upper World and spring water arose from the Under World, the Muscogee kept the two separate with a system of rules and **rituals**. The Muscogee highly **revered** the Great Spirit, also called the Master of Breath.

The most important ceremony was the eight-day, late-summer Green Corn Ceremony held just after the corn crop had ripened. During the ceremony, the

From corn, squash, and wild plants, the women prepared a variety of foods, shown here in a more modern setting. During the Green Corn Ceremony, or Busk, the Muscogee gave thanks for corn, which grew even when other crops failed.

elders, or the oldest people, put out the town fire that had been burning for the entire previous year and lit a new one. This fire was used to light new family fires. Through dance and prayer, the Muscogee gave thanks for the harvest and asked and received forgiveness for any misdeeds.

THE MUSCOGEE NATION TODAY

CHAPTER 10

While the Muscogee (Creek) Nation has more members than ever before, it still faces many challenges. Jobs are scarce in many of the nation's counties. Due to years of little or no access to health care, many people, especially the older ones, suffer from serious health problems such as **diabetes** and high blood pressure.

To address these problems, the Muscogee (Creek) Nation provides a wide array of education, health, and employment services. The nation owns and operates four health clinics and a hospital. The Office of Employment and Training helps people secure job training and jobs, and many Muscogee teenagers find work through the Summer Youth Employment program. They can acquire leadership skills by joining Youth Councils, where Muscogee history and language are also taught. The nation supplies more than twelve hundred **grants** and **scholarships** to Muscogee college students.

Forming the Muscogee National Business **Enterprise** has helped council leaders bring in money from the United States government. These funds support construction, business, and manufacturing projects that provide jobs and services for members of the tribe.

The Muscogee (Creek) Nation owns and operates several cattle farms, three travel plazas, and four bingo halls, including this one in Okmulgee, Oklahoma. Profits help support educational and social services for the nation's members.

MUSCOGEE WRITERS AND ARTISTS

CHAPTER 11

Born in Tulsa, Oklahoma, Muscogee Joy Harjo studied painting, theater, and creative writing. Her many writing awards include the Wordcraft Circle of Native Writers and Storytellers' Writer of the Year award for her children's book, *The Good Luck Cat*. In 2014, she published *Crazy Brave: A Memoir*.

Cynthia Leitich Smith, a member of the Muscogee Nation, loved writing stories while growing up in the 1970s. She has published several children's books, including *Jingle Dancer*, about a **contemporary** Muscogee girl in Oklahoma; *Rain is Not My Indian Name*, about a young photographer becoming active in Native American affairs; and *Indian Shoes*, a collection of short stories about a boy and his grandfather, set in rural Oklahoma and in Chicago.

Some Muscogee have merged their artistic talents with their interests in honoring and keeping Native customs alive. Muscogee artist Martha Noon-Tomah researches how early Muscogee made metal jewelry. She also teaches traditional jewelry-making techniques to young Muscogee.

Dan Townsend is a well-known Muscogee shell carver. He creates medicine cups, pendants, and earrings. Some of his carvings are based on ancient designs from the southeastern United States, while others are original images of animals especially associated with water, such as dolphins, herons, and dragonflies.

(Left) Poet Joy Harjo helped found the Poetic Justice Band. The band combines poetry with tribal, jazz, and rock music. *(Right)* Using imagination, patience, and skill, the Muscogee made traditional beaded bags such as this one.

ACTIVISM

CHAPTER 12

Intent on destroying Native American communities, the U.S. government passed the Indian **Relocation** Act of 1953. Among other things, the act paid bus fares for Native Americans who agreed to move far away from their **reservations** or tribal towns. They also funded job-training programs in the new areas. Many Muscogee young adults left their tribal towns where jobs were scarce, hoping they could prosper in new locations. One such Muscogee was Millie Ketcheschawno.

In Oakland, California, and in San Francisco, Ketcheschawno formed friendships with many other young Native Americans. Throughout the late 1950s and early 1960s, they began reclaiming their traditions.

In 1963, the U.S. government shut down a federal prison on Alcatraz Island, just off the California coast in the San Francisco Bay. In 1969, the San Francisco United Council of Native Americans proposed that Alcatraz be turned into a spiritual and **ecology** center for Indians. When the U.S. government objected, the

Native Americans, including Ketcheschawno, occupied Alcatraz Island. From 1969 to 1971, nearly fifteen thousand Native Americans visited or stayed in Alcatraz. Their **activism** showed that despite many attempts, the U.S. government could not break the many threads that bound Native Americans to a proud history and identity.

This hand-painted sign on Alcatraz Island welcomed Indian occupiers to "United Indian Property." With the occupation, Alcatraz became a symbol of growing Native American power.

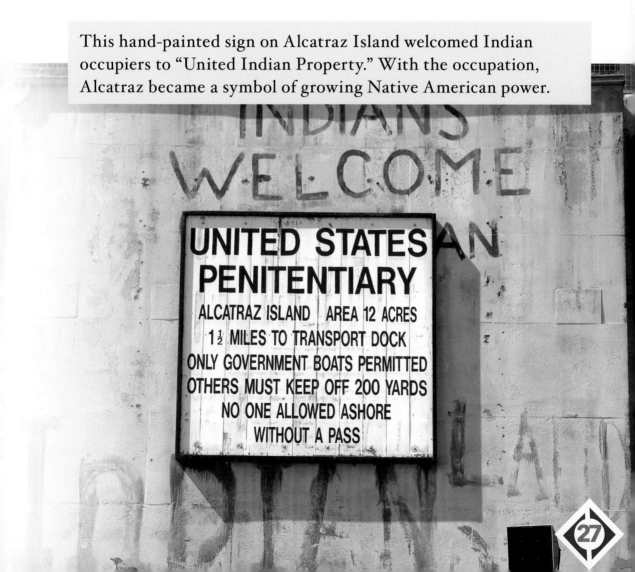

PRESERVATION AND PROGRESS
CHAPTER 13

The leaders of the Muscogee (Creek) Nation work to ensure the well-being of all its members. Nation-sponsored social services reach many people, and new businesses and industries help make the nation's economy healthy and modern.

In 2010, the Muscogee (Creek) Nation bought back its historic tribal **capitol** building, the Council House, from the city of Okmulgee. The Council House is a museum of Muscogee history, hosting exhibitions of Muscogee arts and crafts.

In 2015, the Muscogee (Creek) Nation announced a $22 million plan for RiverWalk Crossing in Jenks, Oklahoma, an entertainment district on the Arkansas River, which will hosts shops, restaurants, family activities, and live music.

The Poarch Band of Creek Indians are trying to develop an interpretative center and memorial garden at Hickory Ground, near Wetumpka, Alabama, the site of an ancient Muscogee town. The interpretative

The Muscogee War Memorial in Okmulgee, Oklahoma, is located near the offices of the Muscogee (Creek) Nation. The war memorial honors veterans from several wars.

center will educate visitors, while the memorial garden will house Muscogee human remains and funeral objects currently in museums across the United States.

Many Muscogee people still keep their traditions. Children, adults, and elders join together in ceremonies to honor their ancestry and nourish their spirits. Despite countless invasions, betrayals, and efforts to destroy them, the Muscogee people remain strong.

GLOSSARY

abundance: A large amount of something.

activism: Acting strongly in support of or against an issue.

capitol: A building in which a government's main lawmaking body meets.

civil war: A war between two groups within a nation.

confederacy: A league of people or states that support each other and act together.

constitution: The basic laws by which a country, state, or group is governed.

contemporary: Modern.

culture: The arts, beliefs, and customs that form a people's way of life.

diabetes: A disorder that causes the body to produce too much urine and causes high levels of sugar in the blood.

ecology: A science that deals with the relationships between groups of living things and their surroundings.

enterprise: A business organization.

grant: An amount of money given to someone by a government or company to be used for a certain purpose.

insulate: To prevent heat, electricity, or sound from passing through.

nation: People who have their own customs, laws, and land separate from other nations or people.

regiment: A military unit made of several large groups of soldiers.

relocation: The act of moving to a new place.

reservation: Land set aside by the government for specific Native American tribes to live on.

revere: To have great respect for something.

ritual: A formal ceremony.

scholarship: Money given for education.

FOR MORE INFORMATION

BOOKS

Dwyer, Helen, and Amy Stone. *Creek History and Culture.* New York, NY: Gareth Stevens Publishing, 2011.

Gibson, Karen Bush. *Native American History for Kids: With 21 Activities.* Chicago, IL: Chicago Review Press, 2010.

Schwartz, Heather E. *Forced Removal: Causes and Effects of the Trail of Tears.* North Mankato, MN: Capstone Press, 2015.

WEBSITES

Due to the changing nature of Internet links, PowerKids Press has developed an online list of websites related to the subject of this book. This site is updated regularly. Please use this link to access the list: www.powerkidslinks.com/sona/musc

INDEX